WORLD ALMANAC

Library of
American
GOVERNMENT

The
BILL OF RIGHTS
AND OTHER AMENDMENTS

BY GEOFFREY M. HORN

WORLD ALMANAC® LIBRARY

Please visit our web site at: www.worldalmanaclibrary.com
For a free color catalog describing World Almanac® Library's list
of high-quality books and multimedia programs, call 1-800-848-2928 (USA)
or 1-800-387-3178 (Canada). World Almanac® Library's fax: (414) 332-3567.

Library of Congress Cataloging-in-Publication Data

Horn, Geoffrey M.
    The Bill of Rights and other amendments / by Geoffrey M. Horn.
        p. cm. — (World Almanac Library of American government)
    Includes bibliographical references and index.
    ISBN 0-8368-5475-6 (lib. bdg.)
    ISBN 0-8368-5480-2 (softcover)
    Contents: An unfinished document — The First Amendment — Other fundamental freedoms —The Justice System — States'
rights, slavery, and the civil war — Changing the way government works — Expanding democracy.
    1. United States, Constitution, 1st-10th Amendments—Juvenile literature. 2. Constitutional amendments—United
States—Juvenile literature. 3. Civil rights—United States—Juvenile literature. [1. United States, Constitution, 1st-10th
Amendments. 2. Constitutional amendments—United States. 3. Civil rights.] I. Title. II. Series.
    KF4750.H67   2003
    342.73'085—dc21   2003052596

First published in 2004 by
World Almanac® Library
330 West Olive Street, Suite 100
Milwaukee, WI 53212 USA

Copyright © 2004 by World Almanac® Library.

Project editor: Alan Wachtel
Project manager: Jonny Brown
Cover design and layout: Melissa Valuch
Photo research: Diane Laska-Swanke
Indexer: Walter Kronenberg
Production: Beth Meinholz

Photo credits: © AP/Wide World Photos: 18, 19 both, 20, 21, 23, 24, 25, 29, 31, 34; © Bettmann/CORBIS: 4 top, 5, 7,
10, 37, 39 bottom; Courtesy National Archives and Records Administration: cover (background), title page, 8;
© Charles Gupton/CORBIS: 14 bottom; © Chris Hondros/Getty Images: 9; © Hulton Archive/Getty Images: 11 bottom,
14 top, 15, 26, 27, 28 top, 32, 33, 35, 38; © James Keivom/Getty Images: 16; © Michael Keza/Getty Images: 13;
© Chris Martinez/Getty Images: 17; © David McNew/Getty Images: 22 bottom; © North Wind Picture Archives: 28
bottom; © Owaki – Kulla/CORBIS: 4 bottom; © Bill Pugliano/Getty Images: 22 top; © Royalty-Free/CORBIS: 6;
© Mike Simons/Getty Images: 11 top; © Leif Skoogfors/CORBIS: 39 top; © Mark L. Stephenson/CORBIS: cover (main)

Printed in the United States of America

1 2 3 4 5 6 7 8 9 07 06 05 04 03

About the Author

GEOFFREY M. HORN is a freelance writer and editor with a lifelong interest in politics and
the arts. He is the author of books for young people and adults, and has contributed hundreds of articles
to encyclopedias and other reference books, including *The World Almanac*. He lives in southwestern
Virginia, in the foothills of the Blue Ridge Mountains, with his wife, four cats (at last count), and one
rambunctious collie. He dedicates this book to his sister Maddy and to the memory of Annie, Rosie, and
Elizabeth (Libby) Laderman.

TABLE OF CONTENTS

Words that appear in the glossary are printed in **boldface** type the first time they occur in the text.

Chapter One

AN UNFINISHED DOCUMENT

▲ In colonial times, downtown New York City had wooden buildings instead of steel, glass, and concrete skyscrapers, and horse-drawn wagons instead of buses, taxis, and cars.

When the **framers** of the Constitution met in 1787 in Philadelphia, Pennsylvania, most of America was wilderness, and the country had a total population of less than four million. Today, the United States extends from the Atlantic to the Pacific and is home to more than two hundred and ninety million people. Computers, video games, cell phones, shopping malls, superhighways, jet planes, space satellites—these are all routine aspects of American life that the framers could hardly have imagined.

As the nation has changed, so have people's ideas about freedom. In the late eighteenth century, the only people allowed to vote in most states were white males over the age of twenty-one. Slaves in many states could be bought, sold, and used like property. Few women could vote or run for public office. No country that allowed such unfair treatment would be called free today.

◤ The development of huge shopping malls is just one of many ways the nation has changed since the Constitution was written.

AMENDING THE CONSTITUTION

Although the framers could not foresee exactly how much the nation would grow, they understood the need for the Constitution to grow along with it. For this reason, they provided ways to make changes, or **amendments**, to the original document.

◀ In the nineteenth century, Sojourner Truth worked to end slavery, raise the status of women, and deepen the nation's commitment to freedom and justice for all people.

Procedures for amending the Constitution are set out in Article V. The most commonly used method requires a proposed amendment to pass Congress by at least a two-thirds vote in both the House of Representatives and the Senate. If approved by Congress, the amendment is then sent to the state legislatures. When the proposed amendment has been **ratified** by three-fourths of the state legislatures, it then becomes part of the Constitution. Twenty-six of the Constitution's twenty-seven amendments have been ratified in this manner.

Instead of sending the proposed amendment to the state legislatures, Congress may require that a separate convention be held in each state. This procedure was used in ratifying the original Constitution. For amending the Constitution this method has been used only once—to ratify the Twenty-first Amendment, which ended **Prohibition**. (See Chapter 6.)

Article V also outlines yet another very different method for amending the Constitution. Under this method, if two-thirds of the state legislatures request it, Congress must call a national constitutional convention. Amendments approved by

Amendments by the Numbers

More than ten thousand constitutional amendments have been introduced in Congress since 1789. Of these, only thirty-three passed Congress, and only twenty-seven were ratified by enough states to become law.

In December 1791, when only fourteen states belonged to the Union, approval by eleven states was needed to ratify a constitutional amendment. Today, thirty-eight of the fifty states are needed to ratify.

such a national convention would then be submitted either to the state legislatures or to separate state conventions. Each amendment ratified by three-fourths of the states would then become law. This method for amending the Constitution has never been used.

THE FIRST TEN AMENDMENTS

Even before the final draft of the Constitution was approved and signed in 1787, delegates from some states were

Facts About the Constitution

Fifty-five delegates to the Constitutional Convention began formal meetings in Philadelphia on May 25, 1787. Thirty-nine of them signed the final draft of the Constitution on September 17.

The Constitution was ratified when New Hampshire—the ninth of the original thirteen states—gave its approval on June 21, 1788. The document came into effect on March 4, 1789.

The original text of the Constitution consists of an introduction, or preamble, and seven major sections, called articles. Article I describes the House of Representatives and the Senate. Article II deals with the president, and Article III discusses the Supreme Court and lower courts.

▲ **Independence Hall, Philadelphia**

Relations between the **federal government** and the states form the basis of Article IV. Ways of amending the Constitution are outlined in Article V. Article VI proclaims the Constitution as the "supreme Law of the Land," and Article VII describes the procedure for ratification.

The original text of the Constitution is followed by twenty-seven amendments—the main subject of this book. The first ten amendments are known as the **Bill of Rights**. These were ratified in 1791.

The next seventeen amendments were ratified between 1795 and 1992. These additional amendments ended slavery, guaranteed women the right to vote, lowered the national voting age to eighteen, and made the country more democratic in many other ways.

demanding major changes to it. The major objection concerned the lack of a bill of rights—a section protecting every citizen against government abuses. As early as 1776, the state of Virginia had adopted a Declaration of Rights. By 1787, similar declarations had become part of most state constitutions. Typical of such statements were provisions guaranteeing freedom of speech, freedom of the press, and the right to trial by jury.

Some of the framers believed that because most state constitutions already had a bill of rights, the federal Constitution did not need one. They further argued that since nothing in the Constitution gave Congress the power to limit basic freedoms, adding a statement to the Constitution to protect such freedoms was unnecessary.

Whatever their merits, arguments like these changed the minds of very few critics. George Mason—the author of Virginia's Declaration of Rights—refused to sign the Constitution because it had no bill of rights. Writing from Europe, Thomas Jefferson told James Madison that a bill of rights "is what the people are entitled to against every government on earth…and what no government should refuse.…" Many states agreed to ratify the Constitution only after it became clear that Congress would draft a bill of rights and submit it to the states as soon as possible.

The Constitution took effect on March 4, 1789. On September 25, Congress approved and submitted to the states a total of twelve amendments. During the next twenty-seven months, only ten of these amendments were ratified by enough states to become law. Following ratification by the Virginia state legislature on December 15, 1791, these ten amendments—the Bill of Rights—became part of the Constitution.

▲ **Elizabeth Cady Stanton was a leader in the fight to guarantee women the right to vote. The Nineteenth Amendment became law in 1920, eighteen years after her death.**

The Two Missing Amendments

A peculiar history surrounds the two amendments that did not become part of the Constitution in 1791. One amendment—actually the first of the twelve to be submitted—dealt with the future makeup of the House of Representatives. This amendment was promptly abandoned after the Bill of Rights became law.

The other amendment—the second of the twelve—said that any measure passed by Congress to raise its own pay could not take effect until after a congressional election. This amendment, too, might have been completely forgotten if it had not been for the efforts of Gregory Watson, a twenty-year-old student at the University of Texas. While looking for a term paper topic in 1982, Watson came upon the text of the congressional pay-raise amendment. Since the amendment did not include any time limit for ratification, Watson argued that the states could still ratify it if they chose to.

Watson's arguments failed to convince his college professor, who gave him a C on the paper. He had better luck when he wrote to members of the state legislatures telling them about his discovery. This was a time of rising public anger at Congress, which many voters viewed as overpaid, ineffective, and corrupt. State legislators saw a vote in favor of the old amendment as an easy way to respond to the public mood. Amazingly, the restriction on congressional pay raises was ratified as the Twenty-seventh Amendment on May 7, 1992, more than two hundred years after it was first proposed.

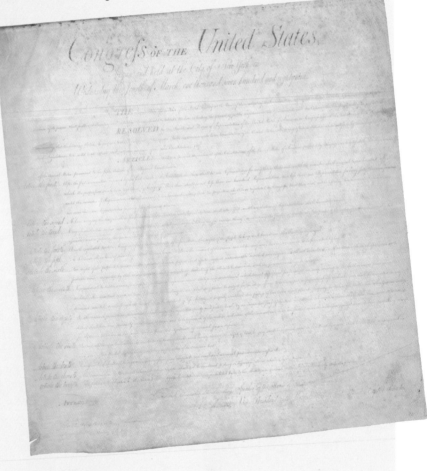

▲ **Bill of Rights**

Chapter Two

THE FIRST AMENDMENT

In a mere forty-five words, the First Amendment to the Constitution guarantees many of the rights that Americans hold most dear:

> *Congress shall make no law respecting an establishment of religion, or prohibiting the free exercise thereof; or abridging the freedom of speech, or of the press; or the right of the people peaceably to assemble, and to petition the Government for a redress of grievances.*

Taken in the broadest sense, the First Amendment bars the government from interfering with:

- Your right to practice your own religion, or no religion;
- Your right to say what you think;
- Your right to publish and read your choice of books, newspapers, or magazines;
- Your right to gather peacefully to protest unjust laws and policies.

When the First Amendment was proposed in 1789, it had a narrower meaning than it has today. The first five words—*"Congress shall make no law…"*—sent a clear signal that the amendment applied only to actions of the federal government. Not until the Fourteenth Amendment was ratified in 1868 did the federal Bill of Rights clearly apply to many actions by state and local governments. (See Chapter 5.)

LIMITS ON THE FIRST AMENDMENT

In practice, your rights under the First Amendment are not as absolute as they might seem. Laws passed by Congress and decisions

▼ **These Muslims are using their First Amendment freedoms by studying and praying at a mosque in Queens, New York.**

The Constitution and the Supreme Court

Since the early nineteenth century, the Supreme Court has been the main guardian and interpreter of the Constitution. The Court interprets the meaning of the Constitution by resolving disputes that have worked their way up from lower courts. The name of a case—for example, *New York Times v. Sullivan*—always shows the names of the people or organizations involved in the dispute. The "*v.*" in the middle stands for *versus*, a Latin word meaning "against."

made by the Supreme Court have recognized limits on all the freedoms listed in the Bill of Rights.

For example, the First Amendment does not give you the right to say or print hurtful things about people when you know the statements are untrue. It does not give you the right to say or show things to other people for the purpose of threatening or harassing them. It does not give you the right to make false and misleading claims about a product you want to sell. Nor does it give you the right to say or print anything that might pose a "clear and present danger" to others. In the words of Oliver Wendell Holmes, a famous Supreme Court justice, the First Amendment "would not protect a man in falsely shouting fire in a theatre and causing a panic."

▼ **The First Amendment protects the right to protest peacefully. These demonstrators are protesting the Supreme Court decision that made abortion legal.**

Full rights under the First Amendment apply only to adults. The law gives parents a great deal of leeway in deciding what their children may or may not read, and where and how they must worship. To maintain order and discipline, school officials may also limit their students' First Amendment rights—for example, by censoring articles written by staff members of a school-sponsored student newspaper.

As with other rights, however, the powers of parents and school officials are not absolute. As the Supreme Court held in a 1969 decision, students do not "shed their constitutional rights to freedom of speech or expression at the schoolhouse gate."

FREEDOM OF RELIGION

The part of the First Amendment that deals with religion is known as the **Establishment Clause**. It is one thing that separates the United States from countries like Great Britain, which have established a national church. In Britain, the king or queen heads the Church of England and appoints its highest officials. Two archbishops and twenty-four senior bishops sit as members

⚠ Courts have been asked to decide whether this Ohio high school and other public schools may display the biblical Ten Commandments on school grounds.

Unpopular Causes

The First Amendment protects people's rights to express their views, regardless of how unpopular or outrageous those views might be. A remarkable—and very controversial—example of this is the decision by the Supreme Court in *United States v. Eichman* (1990) to overturn the Flag Protection Act. This law, passed by Congress in 1989, made it a crime for any protester to burn, mutilate, or otherwise mistreat the American flag.

Writing for the majority in the *Eichman* case, Justice William J. Brennan, Jr., said: "If there is a bedrock principle underlying the First Amendment, it is that the Government may not prohibit the expression of an idea simply because society finds the idea itself offensive or disagreeable."

⚠ Protesters in Washington, D.C., burned a U.S. flag while demonstrating against the Vietnam War in 1969.

of the House of Lords. The First Amendment forbids the establishment of any national church in the United States.

The framers were not hostile to religion, but they were wary of entangling religious influence with political power. They knew that many Europeans had come to America to escape religious persecution. They wanted to build, as Thomas Jefferson said, "a wall of separation between church and state." The framers underlined their concerns not only in the First Amendment but also in Article VI of the main body of the Constitution. Article VI says that "no religious Test shall ever be required" as a condition for holding government office.

Like other ideas built into the Constitution, the wall of separation between church and state is not absolute. "Under God" is part of the Pledge of Allegiance. "In God We Trust" appears on every dollar bill. Congress starts its work each day with a prayer, and the Supreme Court begins each public session with the words "God save the United States and this Honorable Court!"

If religious belief is so closely woven into the fabric of American society, how can we determine when a particular practice violates the Establishment Clause? In recent decades the Supreme Court has developed three tests to decide such issues. The first test is whether a particular practice improperly favors or promotes one particular religion over another. The second test is whether people are pressured in some way to take part in a religious observance they might otherwise prefer to avoid.

The third test is known as the "Lemon test" because it comes from the Court's decision in a 1971 case, *Lemon v. Kurtzman*. In *Lemon*, the Court was asked to decide whether public money can go to religious schools. The answer is yes, but only if three conditions are met. First, the law allowing the aid must have a valid **secular**, or non-religious, purpose. Second, its main effect must be "one that neither advances nor inhibits religion." Third, it must not go too far in entangling government with religion. In practice, while keeping the "Lemon test," the Court has taken an increasingly lenient view of public aid to religious schools in recent years.

The justices have likewise become more tolerant of prayer in the public schools. In *Good News Club v. Milford Central School* (2001), the Court ruled that if a school allowed secular groups to meet on school grounds, it must allow prayer groups the same freedom. The Court has also held that states may require schools to observe a "moment of silence"—a moment that some students may use as a time for private prayer.

FREEDOM OF THE PRESS

Reporters dig up scandals, uncover government corruption, and publish embarrassing secrets that many people would rather keep hidden. For these reasons, among others, reporters and the newspapers they work for are not always popular. The framers understood the need for a free press to keep the government from abusing power—although, like today's politicians, they often took a dim view of what the newspapers said about them.

The free press provision of the First Amendment has been greatly strengthened by two important Supreme Court decisions. The first decision, *New York Times v. Sullivan* (1964), dealt with a claim by a public official that the *Times*, one of the nation's great newspapers, had **libeled** him by publishing an advertisement that contained false information about him. In fact, some of the information *was* false, but the Court held that this was not enough to force the *Times* to pay damages. Instead, the Court said,

▼ Like newspapers, TV news networks are protected by the First Amendment.

▲ Publication of the Pentagon Papers by the *New York Times* was a landmark in the history of freedom of the press.

a public official suing for libel must prove that the newspaper acted with "actual malice"—that is, while fully knowing that the statement was false or "with reckless disregard of whether it was true or false."

The Court delivered another forceful blow in favor of freedom of the press in *New York Times v. United States* (1971), usually known as the Pentagon Papers case. The Pentagon Papers is a secret history of the Vietnam War. It showed that United States government officials had not been honest about when and how the United States had become involved in Vietnam. This secret history was leaked to the *Times* by Daniel Ellsberg, a former Defense Department employee. Claiming that release of the Pentagon Papers harmed national security, government officials tried to stop the *Times* from publishing the documents, but the Supreme Court said no. It refused to allow the government to violate the First Amendment by censoring the press.

The First Amendment and the Internet

Many press freedom cases have dealt with newspapers, but the First Amendment also applies to books, magazines, movies, videos, songs, radio and television broadcasts, and the Internet.

In 1996, Congress passed the Communications Decency Act, in order to shield young people from harmful materials on the Internet. The following year, in *Reno v. American Civil Liberties Union*, the Supreme Court ruled that some parts of this law were so broad they violated the First Amendment. "Regulation of the content of speech," said the Court, "is more likely to interfere with the free exchange of ideas than to encourage it. The interest in encouraging freedom of expression in a democratic society outweighs any theoretical but unproven benefit of censorship."

▲ First Amendment freedoms apply to the Internet, the Supreme Court has ruled.

OTHER FUNDAMENTAL FREEDOMS

The framers were no strangers to war. Nearly all the delegates had taken an active part in the American Revolution, and many had commanded troops in the Continental Army. They knew that war could wreck the lives of civilians as well as soldiers. But they also knew that the young nation would not survive if the national government lacked the means to defend itself against its enemies.

Two provisions in the Bill of Rights—the Second Amendment and the Third Amendment—deal specifically with the relationship between soldiers and citizens. Of these two, the Second Amendment has attracted far

▲ The Second Amendment has its roots in colonial times, when militias like these Massachusetts "minutemen" had to be ready to fight at a moment's notice.

The Bill of Rights—A Basic Outline

The first ten amendments to the Constitution are known as the Bill of Rights. These amendments are:

Amendment I: Freedom of religion, speech, press, and assembly.
Amendment II: Right to keep and bear arms.
Amendment III: Protection against military abuses.
Amendment IV: Protection from unreasonable search and seizure.
Amendment V: Right to fair treatment in legal cases.
Amendment VI: Right to a speedy, fair, and public trial.
Amendment VII: Right to trial by jury in many civil cases.
Amendment VIII: Protection against cruel and unusual punishments.
Amendment IX: Rights retained by the people.
Amendment X: Powers reserved to the states.

greater attention. In fact, it is more hotly disputed today than it was two centuries ago.

THE SECOND AMENDMENT

The Second Amendment reads, in full:

> *A well regulated Militia, being necessary to the security of a free State, the right of the people to keep and bear Arms, shall not be infringed.*

The first four words of the amendment call for some explanation. In the main body of the Constitution, the framers gave Congress the power to "raise and support Armies," and they made the president the commander in chief of the armed forces. The framers, however, did not want the federal government to maintain a large standing army. Instead, in wartime, they expected all able-bodied men to take up their weapons and join **militias**—groups of armed citizens. The tasks of organizing and training the militias were left to the states.

Some scholars think the framers meant the Second Amendment mainly as a way to keep the federal government from dismantling the state militias. In this view, the amendment protects the rights of state militia members against interference by the federal government, though not from regulation by state governments. Other scholars argue that the main thrust of the amendment is to safeguard the rights of individual citizens to buy, own, and carry their own weapons. This way of reading the amendment is the one that today's defenders of gun rights favor.

Like all other rights in the Bill of Rights, the right "to keep and bear Arms" is not absolute. The Second Amendment does not allow

▼ **At a memorial in Littleton, Colorado, Columbine High School students mourn the victims of a 1999 rampage in which fifteen people died. The killings focused renewed attention on the threat of gun violence.**

you to carry a loaded gun to school or set up a rocket-propelled grenade launcher in your backyard. In *United States v. Miller* (1939) and later decisions, the Supreme Court has upheld various limits on the kinds of weapons Americans may legally own and carry. Different states have different laws regarding the right to keep and bear arms.

Gun Rights and Gun Control

According to a recent survey, the United States has more than 230 million firearms—far more than any other country in the world. About 98 percent of these weapons are in the hands of private citizens. In the 1990s, the Centers for Disease Control and Prevention, a federal agency, compared figures about gun violence in the United States with those for twenty-five other major countries, including Australia, Canada, England, France, Germany, Italy, and Japan. The agency found that American children, on average, were sixteen times more likely to be murdered with a gun, eleven times more likely to commit suicide with a gun, and nine times more likely to die from a gun-related accident than children in all the other countries combined.

⬆ **Many weapons are bought and sold at weekend gun shows, which attract thousands of visitors.**

Armed with statistics like these, groups such as Handgun Control and the Coalition to Stop Gun Violence have called for new gun control measures. Many police groups have also joined the campaign. Different organizations favor different plans. Proposals include imposing tighter controls on gun sales, requiring gun-safety courses for gun buyers, childproofing all new handguns, and making all owners of handguns register their weapons.

On the other side of the debate are defenders of gun rights, including the National Rifle Association. They point out that the vast majority of gun owners in the United States are law-abiding citizens who use their guns for hunting or to protect themselves and their homes from attack. Defenders of gun rights oppose new gun control measures. They have also persuaded some state legislatures to pass new laws that expand the rights of gun owners to carry concealed weapons in public places.

The debate over gun rights and gun control is sure to continue in Congress, in the state legislatures, in the courts, and at the ballot box for decades to come.

▲ **Police remove weapons found in a drug raid at a home in Topeka, Kansas. The Fourth Amendment requires police to get a warrant before they can search a house for evidence of lawbreaking.**

"A MAN'S HOUSE"

The belief that "a man's house is his castle" has a long history in England. This idea was beautifully expressed in 1763 by William Pitt, who said:

> The poorest man may, in his cottage, bid defiance to all the forces of the Crown. It may be frail; its roof may shake; the wind may blow through it; the storm may enter; the rain may enter; but the King of England may not enter.

However lovely in principle, this idea was not widely followed in England or colonial America. Government had the power to station troops in people's homes without asking and to search anyone's house for little or no reason.

The Third Amendment limits the power of the government to place soldiers in private homes. It says that while the nation is at peace, the government may not quarter, or station, soldiers in a private home without the homeowner's agreement. This amendment stems from the British practice of commandeering American colonists' homes so that British troops could enforce the tax laws. In fact, "quartering large Bodies of Armed Troops among us" was one of the specific complaints raised against the British crown in the Declaration of Independence of 1776.

SEARCH AND SEIZURE

The specific issues raised in the Third Amendment were very important to the framers but have little bearing on American life today. The Fourth Amendment, on the other hand, raises questions about police power that are as important today as they were in the eighteenth century.

The Fourth Amendment states that the government may not violate the people's right "to be secure in their persons, houses, papers, and effects, against unreasonable searches and seizures." Simply put, it means that before the police can enter your home, they must have:

- Good reason ("probable cause") to believe that you have committed a crime or that your home contains specific evidence of that crime.

- A **search warrant** that clearly states what the police are looking for and where they expect to find it.

⬛ **Police may search a vehicle if they have good reason to suspect illegal activity. These officers stopped a speeding van and found marijuana in the gas tank.**

What happens when evidence is taken without probable cause or a proper warrant? The simple answer is that this evidence must be excluded from trial—that is, it cannot be used against the accused person. This principle is known as the **exclusionary rule**. It was given full force by the Supreme Court in *Mapp v. Ohio* (1961).

Opinions about the exclusionary rule are sharply divided. On the one hand, it offers a potent tool to make sure that police act properly. On the other hand, it means that some cases against dangerous criminals must be dropped because the evidence against them is tainted. To avoid letting too

⬛ **Remote control cameras allow police to monitor trouble spots from miles away.**

many lawbreakers avoid punishment, the Supreme Court since *Mapp* has eased some restrictions on the police. For example, if the police acted in good faith or would have discovered the evidence anyway, the seized material may be used in court even if the search warrant was faulty.

Chapter Four

THE JUSTICE SYSTEM

Five of the ten amendments in the Bill of Rights deal in some way with the rights of people accused of crimes or involved in legal disputes. At first, this might seem surprising. A large majority of people obey the law. Most people rarely see the inside of a courtroom. Why, then, does the document that safeguards the rights of all Americans focus so much on the rights of the few?

Some experts believe the answer to that question, like so much else in the Constitution, can be found in English history. Until the mid-seventeenth century, a special court sat in the royal palace of Westminster, in London. This court was known as the Court of Star Chamber because of the stars on the ceiling of the room where it met. Aides hand-picked by the monarch served as both judge and jury.

The Court of Star Chamber met in secret and had the power to impose fines, prison sentences, whippings, and other more gruesome physical punishments on anyone who was found guilty. Some of the harshest punishments were reserved for those who spoke out in opposition to the government. Although the Court of Star Chamber no longer exists, dictators in other parts of the world still use tactics like these to crush dissent.

The framers never wanted to see anything like the Court of Star Chamber set up in the United States. They wanted to make sure the nation's courts worked fairly and respected the rights guaranteed under the First Amendment. They also wanted to

▼ "Death row" is where prisoners wait to be executed. The Supreme Court has ruled that the death penalty does not violate the Eighth Amendment ban on "cruel and unusual punishments."

make sure that police officers, judges, and other law enforcement officials would not abuse their powers.

TRIAL BY JURY

One of the main ways the Bill of Rights tries to protect people's rights is by use of a jury. The framers strongly believed that jurors—who were chosen from among the people—were more likely to protect people's rights than would judges acting alone.

Major criminal cases involve two kinds of juries. The first kind of jury, known as a grand jury, is discussed in the Fifth Amendment. The grand jury, which usually has twenty-three members, looks at the facts and decides whether there is enough evidence to bring a case to trial. The framers hoped that use of a grand jury might prevent

Security and Freedom

On September 11, 2001, terrorists hijacked four airplanes. Two were deliberately crashed into the twin towers of the World Trade Center. The third smashed into the Pentagon, and the fourth went down in a field in Pennsylvania. In all, more than 3,000 people were killed.

In response, Congress passed laws allowing the United States government to use secret search warrants to spy on suspected terrorists. The government has claimed that it has the right to arrest and hold certain people without detailing the charges against them, allowing them to see a lawyer, or letting their families and friends know where they are.

▲ **Soldiers from the Army National Guard protect against terrorism at a New Jersey airport.**

These practices violate the Bill of Rights. Some people believe this is all right because the nation is at war and because terrorism poses a grave threat to the country. They say the government is correct in curbing the rights of a few people in order to protect the safety of the many. Opponents argue that the new laws are wrong because they weaken the freedoms that are the real strength of the United States.

The new measures are being debated in the media, the Congress, and the courts. In time, the Supreme Court will need to define the proper balance between security and freedom.

Marshall Mathers (left), known worldwide as the rap artist Eminem, faced the U.S. court system when he was arrested in 2000 on weapons charges. After pleading no contest, he was put on probation and required to perform community service.

overzealous government officials from harassing innocent people by bringing cases based on flimsy evidence.

The second kind of jury is known as a trial jury or, sometimes, as a petit (or petty) jury. This is the kind of jury most people are familiar with. In the United States, it usually has twelve members. In criminal cases, the trial jury must decide whether someone is guilty or innocent of a crime. In civil cases, the trial jury must decide disputes between private citizens or organizations.

DUE PROCESS

The Fifth Amendment says that no one may "be deprived of life, liberty, or property, without due process of law." **Due process** is a legal term that means fair treatment under the law. The term is very broad and embraces many kinds of legal rights, including the right to trial by jury. Here are some of the due process rights specifically mentioned in the Bill of Rights:

- Fourth Amendment—Forbids unreasonable searches and seizures (see Chapter 3).
- Fifth Amendment—Prevents the government from putting someone on trial twice for the

Demonstrators protest the fatal shooting in 2002 of Gonzalo Martinez in Downey, California. Martinez, who was unarmed, was killed after a car chase by police wielding handguns and a machine gun.

Rights of Crime Victims

In the 1960s, several Supreme Court decisions strengthened the rights of people accused of crimes. These decisions provoked fierce opposition, especially from Americans who thought that not enough attention was being paid to the rights and needs of crime victims.

Since then, the federal and state governments have moved to remedy the situation. Today, all states have laws protecting crime victims, and most states have amended their constitutions to provide for victims' rights. Programs have been set up to help crime victims, including domestic violence shelters and rape crisis centers.

▲ **President Bill Clinton (right) signed the federal "Megan's Law" in 1996.**

The victims' rights movement won an important victory in 2003, when the Supreme Court upheld state laws that allow families to find out when a sex offender is living in their neighborhood. Such laws, known as "Megan's Laws," are named for Megan Kanka, a seven-year-old who was killed in 1994 by a man who had previously been convicted of sex offenses against children.

same crime, forcing people to give evidence against themselves in a criminal case, or taking private property without paying the property owner.

- Sixth Amendment—Guarantees to people who are accused of crimes the right to a speedy, public, and fair trial; the right to know what they are accused of; and the right to hear and question the witnesses against them.
- Seventh Amendment—Provides for a jury trial in many civil cases.

Double Jeopardy

Putting someone on trial twice for the same crime is called **double jeopardy**. This practice is barred by the Fifth Amendment. The ban only applies if the first trial comes to a verdict. If no decision is reached in a first trial, the person accused of the crime may be tried again.

- Eighth Amendment—Bars the government from imposing excessive **bail**, unreasonably heavy fines, or "cruel and unusual punishments."

The Eighth Amendment prohibits the kind of tortures that were imposed by the Court of Star Chamber. It also requires that the punishment fit the crime. For example, most people would agree that a robber with a gun who steals millions of dollars from a bank should get a lengthy prison sentence, but a hungry person who takes a loaf of bread from a grocery store should be punished more lightly.

The Death Penalty and the Eighth Amendment

Thirty-eight states allow use of the death penalty to punish people who commit murder. Between 1977 and 2002 a total of 820 convicted killers were executed—289 of them in Texas alone.

The United States is one of the few democracies in the world that still uses the death penalty. In most European countries, punishing criminals by executing them is considered a violation of human rights.

Defenders of the death penalty say execution is a fitting punishment for taking someone's life and that it helps deter others from committing murder. Opponents say that killing people is wrong, whether the killing is done by violent criminals or by the government. They note that a person who is put in prison by mistake can be released, but if someone is executed by mistake, the error can never be undone.

The Supreme Court has held that, if fairly enforced, the death penalty does not violate the Eighth Amendment ban on cruel and unusual punishments. But the Court has also used the Eighth Amendment to limit when and how the death penalty may be applied. In *Atkins v. Virginia* (2002), for example, the Court reversed an earlier ruling and decided that states may not execute murderers who are mentally retarded.

⬧ Sister Helen Prejean, a leading opponent of the death penalty, addresses a rally in Harrisburg, Pennsylvania. Her best-selling book *Dead Man Walking* has been turned into a film and an opera.

STATES' RIGHTS, SLAVERY, AND THE CIVIL WAR

The framers believed in limited government. They wanted the federal government to have enough power to defend the nation against its enemies, but they also wanted to make sure that the federal government did not become so powerful that it would trample the rights of the people and of the states.

▲ A New Mexico state employee checks the purity of the water in a spring near the Rio Grande.

This principle underlies the Ninth and Tenth amendments— the last two amendments of the Bill of Rights. Put simply, the Ninth Amendment says that the people have rights beyond those that are mentioned in the Bill of Rights or in the main body of the Constitution. For example, the Constitution does not specifically mention the need for a clean and healthy environment. But this does not mean that people do not have a right to breathe clean air and drink pure water.

THE TENTH AMENDMENT

The Tenth Amendment directly addresses the rights of the states. It says that any powers not given specifically to the federal government or specifically denied to the state governments belong to the states or to the people.

This amendment served three purposes. First, it reassured the states that they were not about to be swallowed up by an all-powerful federal government. Second, it set up a system under which both the federal government and the state governments could keep a watchful eye on each other.

Reviving the Ninth Amendment

From the early 1790s through the early 1960s, the Ninth Amendment played only a tiny role in American law. This changed in 1965 when a Supreme Court majority relied partly on the Ninth Amendment in deciding *Griswold v. Connecticut*. The *Griswold* case established a right to privacy—even though the word "privacy" appears nowhere in the Constitution. Since *Griswold*, many hundreds of lawsuits have been filed claiming Ninth Amendment protection for a wide variety of rights.

▼ **To make their forced journeys from Africa to the New World, slaves were brought on board ships, put in shackles, and crowded into the ships' holds.**

This system was designed to make sure that neither state nor federal officials took away rights that properly belonged to the people.

The third purpose of the amendment was to prevent the federal government from intruding into certain issues on which the states could not agree. The most important of these issues was slavery.

During the colonial period, slavery was practiced in the North as well as the South. By the end of the eighteenth century, however, a large majority of the nation's 900,000 black slaves lived in the southern states. Between 1800 and 1860, while opposition to slavery grew in the North, the slave population of the United

The Supreme Court and States' Rights

In recent years the Supreme Court has shown renewed interest in states' rights. Several Court decisions have relied on the Tenth Amendment in order to curb the powers of Congress. The Court has also revived interest in the Eleventh Amendment, which became part of the Constitution in the 1790s. The Eleventh Amendment makes state governments immune from certain types of lawsuits.

States increased to nearly four million. All these slaves lived in the South or in a few slave-holding states that bordered on the South.

THE CIVIL WAR AMENDMENTS

The dispute over slavery was not resolved until the end of the **Civil War**—the bloodiest conflict in the nation's history. Between 1861 and 1865, more than 600,000 American soldiers died. Nearly one out of every five soldiers who fought for the Union did not survive the conflict; for the southern states, the death toll was almost one out of four. Although blacks made up less than one percent of the population of the North, by the end of the war they accounted for about ten percent of the Union army. Nearly 40,000 blacks gave their lives for the Union cause.

The victory of Union forces over the Confederacy in 1865 brought the most far-reaching changes in the United States Constitution since the 1790s. In January 1863, President Abraham Lincoln had issued the Emancipation Proclamation—a decree that freed the slaves in the rebel-

▼ **This illustration shows Confederate troops storming Fort Sanders, Tennessee, in November 1863. Union forces foiled the attack by stretching telegraph wire between tree stumps to slow the southern advance.**

▲ **President Abraham Lincoln signs the Emancipation Proclamation.**

▼ **A *Harper's Weekly* magazine cover from 1867 shows black men in the South casting ballots for the first time.**

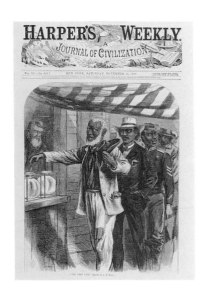

lious southern states. Two years later, Congress passed and the states ratified the Thirteenth Amendment, abolishing slavery through-out the country.

No less important was the Fourteenth Amendment, which was approved by Congress in 1866 and rati-fied by the states in 1868. The Fourteenth Amendment made clear for the first time that every citizen of a particular state was also a full citizen of the whole United States. The Fourteenth Amendment bolstered the Thirteenth by declaring that anyone born in the United States was a U.S. citizen, regard-less of whether that person was born free or as a slave.

Another key provision of the Fourteenth Amendment has had a profound affect on relations between the federal government and the states:

… nor shall any State deprive any person of life, liberty, or property, without due process of law; nor deny to any person within its jurisdiction the equal protection of the laws.

The mention of "due process" in this provision echoes the use of the same term in the Fifth Amendment (see Chapter 4). During the second half of the twentieth century, this part of the Fourteenth Amendment led the Supreme Court to rule that many of the due process guarantees of the federal Bill of Rights must also be applied in state courts.

The part of the provision that guarantees "equal protection of the laws" is known as the **Equal Protection Clause**. It was inserted into the

Constitution to prevent state governments from discriminating against blacks, especially in the South. A famous use of the Equal Protection Clause came in *Brown v. Board of Education* (1954), when the Supreme Court outlawed racial **segregation** in public schools. More recently, the Fourteenth Amendment has been used to break down legal barriers against women and foreigners.

VOTING RIGHTS FOR AFRICAN-AMERICANS

The framers recognized the right to vote as the foundation of the United States government. However, because the framers wanted to limit federal power, they allowed the states to decide who should vote in both state and federal elections. Before the Civil War, the only people who could vote in most states were white males who were over twenty-one years of age.

The abolition of slavery by the Thirteenth Amendment raised this question: would the states that had kept slaves be allowed to bar freed blacks from voting? The answer, said Congress, was no. The reasons were part principle, part politics.

The principle could be seen in the Equal Protection Clause of the Fourteenth Amendment, which was meaning-

▼ Marking a milestone in civil rights history, four black men returned in 1990 to the same Woolworth's lunch counter in Greensboro, North Carolina, where they had been refused service thirty years earlier. The four, who were college students in 1960, had staged a sit-in to protest the store's policy of segregation.

less if blacks were denied the right to vote. The politics came from the fact that most African-Americans at that time supported the Republican Party—the party of Lincoln. Getting as many freed blacks as possible to the polls was not only the right thing to do. It was also in the Republican Party's own interest.

The Fifteenth Amendment—the last of the Civil War amendments—was passed by Congress in 1869 and ratified in 1870. It said that neither the states nor the federal government could bar a former slave from voting or deny anyone the vote because of race or skin color. This should have been the end of the matter, except that Democratic officials in the southern states began to use unfair tactics to keep blacks from voting.

One of these tactics was the **poll tax**—a tax that people had to pay before they would be allowed to vote. The tax was designed to discourage the poorest people, many of whom were black, from even showing up at the polls. The Twenty-fourth Amendment, passed by Congress in 1962 and ratified in 1964, abolished the poll tax in elections for president and members of Congress. Two years later, in *Harper v. Virginia Board of Elections*, the Supreme Court used the Equal Protection Clause to strike down the poll tax in state and local voting.

Letter from the Birmingham City Jail

In 1963, while in jail, the Reverend Martin Luther King, Jr., wrote a letter explaining why African Americans could no longer wait patiently for the equal rights the Constitution promised to all Americans.

We have waited for more than 340 years for our constitutional and God-given rights. The nations of Asia and Africa are moving with jetlike speed toward the goal of political independence, and we still creep at horse and buggy pace toward the gaining of a cup of coffee at a lunch counter. I guess it is easy for those who have never felt the stinging darts of segregation to say "Wait!" But when you have seen vicious mobs lynch your mothers and fathers ... ; when you are humiliated day in and day out by nagging signs reading "white" and "colored"; ... then you will understand why we find it difficult to wait.

CHANGING THE WAY GOVERNMENT WORKS

Some amendments have established great constitutional principles, such as freedom of speech, due process, and equal protection of the laws. Other amendments, such as the one that abolished slavery, have helped to remedy great wrongs. A large number of amendments, however, have been designed to make practical changes in how the government does its job.

▲ The 2000 election highlighted the fact that the U.S. president is not directly chosen by the popular vote, which Al Gore won, but in the electoral college, where George W. Bush (right) came out ahead.

PRESIDENT AND VICE PRESIDENT

One part of the Constitution that has been repeatedly amended is Article II—the part that deals with the election, powers, and term in office of the president and vice president of the United States. Instead of having the people elect the president directly, the framers set up a system in which the people actually vote for members of an electoral college.

Under the framers' original plan, whoever received a majority of votes in the electoral college would become president, and whoever finished second would become vice president. This plan led to a deadlock in the electoral college in 1800, and it took thirty-six ballots in the House of Representatives before Thomas Jefferson was finally elected president over Aaron Burr. The election crisis spurred Congress to revamp the system. Passed in 1803 and ratified a year later, the Twelfth Amendment requires the electors to choose the president and vice president on separate ballots.

▲ **When a president is shot—as Ronald Reagan was in 1981—the attack can have an unsettling effect on the nation as a whole. The Twenty-fifth Amendment eases some of the uncertainty that can follow an assassination attempt by laying out how power is transferred when a president is unable to fulfill the duties of the office.**

The Twentieth Amendment, which was approved in 1932 and ratified in 1933, resolved a constitutional problem that applied both to the president and to Congress. This problem had to do with the long gap between Election Day—the first Tuesday after the first Monday in November—and the time when a newly elected president or member of Congress was scheduled to take office, in early March. (Under Article I of the Constitution, the new Congress was not actually required to meet until the following December, a full thirteen months after the election.) The Twentieth Amendment settled the issue by having the president and vice president begin their terms on January 20. The amendment also sets early January as the time when newly elected members of Congress are sworn in and the new Congress begins to meet.

The framers imposed no limit on the number of four-year terms a president might serve. No president had served more than two terms until Franklin D. Roosevelt, a Democrat, was elected four times. When Republicans took control of Congress in 1947, they vowed to put a cap on how many terms a president could serve. The Twenty-second Amendment, which was ratified in 1951, bars anyone from being elected president more than twice.

As originally written, Article II provided that if the president died in office or was unable to serve for any other reason, the vice president would become president. The office of vice president would then remain vacant until the next presidential and vice presidential election. This issue worried many members of Congress, especially after President John F. Kennedy was killed in 1963 and Vice President

The Unelected President

One oddity of the Twenty-fifth Amendment is that it gave the United States its only president who never won an election either as president or as vice president—Gerald Ford.

Here is what happened: In 1973, Vice President Spiro Agnew resigned because of a bribery scandal. Under the Twenty-fifth Amendment, President Richard Nixon nominated Gerald Ford to replace him. Ford, a popular Republican leader in the House of Representatives, was easily confirmed by Congress.

During this period, Nixon was involved in a huge political scandal—Watergate—and was charged with abusing his powers. When Nixon resigned his office in August 1974, Ford became head of state. The unelected president then used his powers under the Twenty-fifth Amendment to choose an unelected vice president, Nelson Rockefeller, who won congressional approval. Ford ran for a full four-year presidential term in 1976, but was defeated by Jimmy Carter, a Democrat.

⬛ **Neither President Gerald Ford (right) nor his vice president, Nelson Rockefeller, were elected to the offices they assumed in 1974.**

Lyndon B. Johnson—who had serious heart problems—became the nation's head of state. The Twenty-fifth Amendment, passed in 1965 and ratified in 1967, sets up rules for choosing a new vice president after a president dies and the vice president replaces him. The amendment also outlines rules to follow when a president, for whatever reason, is unable to fulfill his duties.

CONGRESS AND THE PEOPLE

Two amendments ratified within ten weeks of each other in 1913 have made a major difference in the way Congress operates. The Sixteenth Amendment, approved by Congress in 1909, legalized the federal income tax. The Seventeenth Amendment, which passed Congress in 1912, changed the way United States senators are elected.

Article I of the Constitution gave Congress the power to collect taxes. But it also said that any "direct taxes" raised

⬛ Because of the Seventeenth Amendment, senators are directly elected by the people of their home states, not by the state legislatures. The photo shows Senator Mary Landrieu of Louisiana celebrating her reelection victory in 2002.

by Congress had to be based on the number of people living in each state, not on how wealthy those taxpayers might be. Using this system, Congress found it hard to raise enough money, especially when the national economy turned sour in the mid-1890s. At the same time, reformers became alarmed about the growing gap between the wealthiest and the poorest Americans.

A solution to both problems was to impose a tax on the incomes of individual taxpayers, regardless of where they lived. If people with big incomes paid a much higher tax rate than people with low incomes, not only would this raise more money for the federal government, but it might also narrow the gap between rich and poor.

Congress passed an income tax law in 1894. The following year, however, the Supreme Court ruled in *Pollock v. Farmers' Loan* that the income tax violated the Constitution. The Sixteenth Amendment, which allowed Congress to tax incomes, successfully overturned the *Pollock* decision. Today, about one of every two dollars collected by the federal government comes from the personal income tax.

The Seventeenth Amendment led to a basic change in the makeup of the Senate. When they wrote the Constitution, the framers had made a clear distinction between the two houses of Congress. They wanted the House of Representatives to respond to the will of the people, and they wanted the Senate to reflect the influence of the states. For this reason, Article I said that senators should be chosen by the state legislatures, not directly elected by the people. The Seventeenth Amendment made Congress more democratic by requiring that senators, like House members, be elected by direct popular vote in their home states.

Prohibition—A Reform That Failed

▲ **Members of the Women's Christian Temperance Union led the fight for Prohibition.**

During the late nineteenth and early twentieth centuries, a growing number of social reformers came to believe that Americans drank far too much liquor. These reformers—many of them women—blamed rum, whiskey, and other alcoholic drinks for what they saw as an alarming rise in crime, violence, and broken homes, especially among poor people and immigrants.

In 1917, Congress passed the Eighteenth Amendment, barring the manufacture, transportation, and sale of liquor. The amendment was ratified in January 1919, and the Prohibition era began a year later.

Prohibition worked—at least for a while. In the early 1920s the saloons were closed, and sales of alcoholic beverages dried up. Within a few years, however, the demand for liquor rose rapidly. Criminals known as bootleggers cashed in on the demand by selling liquor in illegal nightclubs, which were called speakeasies. Profits from bootlegging boosted the incomes of big-time criminals. Some of the money from illegal liquor sales went into the pockets of police officers, who were bribed not to enforce the law.

By the early 1930s, it was clear that Prohibition had failed. In February 1933, Congress passed the Twenty-first Amendment, which repealed the Eighteenth. The Prohibition era ended when the Twenty-first Amendment was ratified that December.

Chapter Seven

EXPANDING DEMOCRACY

The framers understood that every lawful government needed to reflect the will of the people. It is no accident that the Constitution begins "We, the people"—not "We, the states" or "We, the Congress" or "We, the leaders."

At the same time, the framers did not fully trust the people to make wise choices. Many of the framers were worried about the possibility of mob rule—the power of the majority to trample the rights of the minority. Fear of mob rule was one reason why, instead of having the people directly elect all major federal office holders, the framers decided to have the president chosen by an electoral college and the senators chosen by the state legislatures. (See Chapter 6.) The Bill of Rights was a way of protecting individual rights from abuses by the federal government. But it was also a way of shielding individual freedoms from the power of the mob.

Over time, American leaders became less fearful of the power of the mob and more concerned with making the United States as democratic as possible. Several important twentieth-century amendments have done just that.

THE WOMEN'S SUFFRAGE MOVEMENT

The framers did not specifically grant women **suffrage**, meaning the right to vote. But they did not stop women from voting either. Instead, the framers left it up to the states to decide who could vote in local, state, and federal elections. In practice, this meant that very few women were allowed to cast ballots.

One milestone in the suffrage movement was the women's rights convention at Seneca Falls, New York, in 1848. At the insistence of Elizabeth Cady Stanton, one of the convention organizers, the delegates issued a demand for women to have equal voting rights with men—a radical idea at that time. Before the Civil War, many supporters of women's suffrage were also active in the movement to abolish slavery. They were keenly disappointed when the Fifteenth Amendment guaranteed voting rights to former slaves but said nothing at all about voting rights for women. (See Chapter 5.)

▲ **Susan B. Anthony, a champion of women's suffrage.**

In 1872, another women's rights leader, Susan B. Anthony, cast a vote for president, in defiance of New York state law. A judge turned down her claim that she was entitled to vote as a United States citizen under the Fourteenth Amendment. She was fined one hundred dollars but refused to pay. "May it please your honor," she said, "I will never pay a dollar of your unjust penalty....Resistance to tyranny is obedience to God."

Despite many such setbacks. the women's suffrage movement continued to gather strength. The Nineteenth Amendment, which guaranteed women the right to vote in all federal, state, and local elections, was finally passed by Congress in 1919. After a ferocious battle in many state legislatures, the amendment was ratified in time for the presidential election of 1920.

EXTENDING SUFFRAGE

Two more amendments extended voting rights in the 1960s and early 1970s. The Twenty-third Amendment, passed by Congress in 1960 and ratified in 1961, allowed people living in the District of Columbia—also known as Washington, D.C.—the right to vote in presidential elections. The district, which has a population of more than 570,000 people, was given a total of three votes in the electoral college.

The Twenty-third Amendment did not give the District of Columbia the right to elect full voting members of either the House of Representatives or the Senate. An amendment to allow the district to elect one House member and two senators was passed by Congress in 1978. Like the Equal Rights Amendment (see below), it carried a seven-year time limit for ratification. This amendment, too, got bogged down

Whatever Happened to the Equal Rights Amendment?

After the passage of the Nineteenth Amendment, Alice Paul, a suffragist leader, wrote another proposed amendment to the Constitution—the **Equal Rights Amendment**, or ERA. Its purpose was to guarantee women the same legal rights as men. The ERA was introduced in Congress in 1923. Its passage by Congress nearly fifty years later was hailed as a tremendous victory by leaders of the women's rights movement.

When Congress passed the ERA in 1972, it set a time limit of seven years for ratification. This meant that opponents of the ERA could kill the amendment if they could keep enough state legislatures from voting on it. The opponents fought hard, claiming that the ERA would undermine the traditional family and end some legal protections that women already enjoyed.

When it became clear in 1978 that there

▲ The ERA was supported enthusiastically in New York City, where this 1975 rally was held. The amendment, however, was blocked in enough state legislatures to keep it from becoming federal law.

would not be enough time for the required thirty-eight states to ratify the ERA, Congress voted to extend the deadline until 1982. When this deadline also was not met, the ERA failed to become part of the Constitution.

The failure of the ERA did not bring an end to the fight for full legal rights for women. Some rights have been expanded through cases brought under the Equal Protection Clause of the Fourteenth Amendment.

in the state legislatures, and when the deadline passed in 1985, only sixteen states had voted to ratify it.

The Twenty-sixth Amendment, which lowered the nationwide voting age to eighteen, was passed by Congress and ratified by the states in 1971. The time between passage and ratification was less than four months—the shortest for any constitutional amendment. The compelling reason for lowering the voting age was the fact that the nation was in the middle of the Vietnam War, and men as young as eighteen were being drafted to fight overseas. Most people agreed that, as a matter of fairness, any American old enough to risk death while wearing the uniform of the armed forces was old enough to cast a ballot on Election Day.

▲ "Old enough to fight, old enough to vote" was the basic idea behind the Twenty-sixth Amendment.

◀ Three years after the Twenty-third Amendment was ratified, voters in Washington, D.C., waited in long lines to cast their ballots in the 1964 presidential election.

AMENDMENTS TO THE CONSTITUTION

The following are excerpts from the twenty-seven amendments to the United States Constitution, as reprinted in *The World Almanac and Book of Facts 2003*. Some original spellings have been preserved. Boldface text preceding each amendment is a brief summary, added by the editors. Text in italics and brackets, also added by the editors, provides additional information on the amendment.

THE FIRST TEN AMENDMENTS: THE BILL OF RIGHTS
[In force Dec. 15, 1791.]

AMENDMENT I
Religious establishment prohibited. Freedoms of speech, press, assembly.
Congress shall make no law respecting an establishment of religion, or prohibiting the free exercise thereof; or abridging the freedom of speech, or of the press; or the right of the people peaceably to assemble, and to petition the Government for a redress of grievances.

AMENDMENT II
Right to keep and bear arms.
A well regulated Militia, being necessary to the security of a free State, the right of the people to keep and bear Arms, shall not be infringed.

AMENDMENT III
Protection against military abuses.
No Soldier shall, in time of peace be quartered in any house, without the consent of the Owner, nor in time of war, but in a manner to be prescribed by law.

AMENDMENT IV
Protection from unreasonable search and seizure.
The right of the people to be secure in their persons, houses, papers, and effects, against unreasonable searches and seizures, shall not be violated, and no Warrants shall issue, but upon probable cause, supported by Oath or affirmation, and particularly describing the place to be searched, and the persons or things to be seized.

AMENDMENT V
Need for grand jury in major crimes; due process of law; restriction against double jeopardy. Private property not to be taken without compensation.
No person shall be held to answer for a capital, or otherwise infamous crime, unless on a presentment or indictment of a Grand Jury, except in cases arising in the land or naval forces, or in the Militia, when in actual service in time of War or public danger; nor shall any person be subject for the same offence to be twice put in jeopardy of life or limb; nor shall be compelled in any criminal case to be a witness against himself, nor be deprived of life, liberty, or property, without due process of law; nor shall private property be taken for public use, without just compensation.

AMENDMENT VI
Right to speedy trial; witnesses; other criminal rights.
In all criminal prosecutions, the accused shall enjoy the right to a speedy and public trial, by an impartial jury of the State and district wherein the crime shall have been committed, which district shall have been previously ascertained by law, and to be informed of the nature and cause of the accusation; to be confronted with the witnesses against him; to have compulsory process for obtaining witnesses in his favor, and to have the Assistance of Counsel for his defence.

AMENDMENT VII
Right to trial by jury in many civil cases.
In suits at common law, where the value in controversy shall exceed twenty dollars, the right of trial by jury shall be preserved, and no fact tried by a jury, shall be otherwise reexamined in any Court of the United States, than according to the rules of the common law.

AMENDMENT VIII
Ban on excessive bail, excessive fines, and cruel and unusual punishments.
Excessive bail shall not be required, nor excessive fines imposed, nor cruel and unusual punishments inflicted.

AMENDMENT IX
Rights retained by the people.
The enumeration in the Constitution, of certain rights, shall not be construed to deny or disparage others retained by the people.

AMENDMENT X
Powers reserved to the states.
The powers not delegated to the United States by the Constitution, nor prohibited by it to the States, are reserved to the States respectively, or to the people.

AMENDMENTS SINCE THE BILL OF RIGHTS

AMENDMENT XI
Limits on lawsuits against the states.
The Judicial power of the United States shall not be construed to extend to any suit in law or equity, commenced or prosecuted against one of the United States by Citizens of another State, or by Citizens or Subjects of any Foreign State.

[This amendment was proposed to the legislatures of the several states by the Third Congress on March. 4, 1794, and was declared to have been ratified in a message from the president to Congress, dated Jan. 8, 1798. As a result of later research in the Department of State, it is now established that Amendment XI became part of the Constitution on Feb. 7, 1795, for on that date it had been ratified by the required twelve states.]

AMENDMENT XII
Choosing the president and vice president.
[Proposed by Congress, Dec. 9, 1803; ratified, June 15, 1804.]
The Electors shall meet in their respective states and vote by ballot for President and Vice-President, one of whom, at least, shall not be an inhabitant of the same state with themselves; they shall name in their ballots the person voted for as President, and in distinct ballots the person voted for as Vice-President, and they shall make distinct lists of all persons voted for as President, and of all persons voted for as Vice-President, and of the number of votes for each, which lists they shall sign and certify, and transmit sealed to the seat of the government of the United States, directed to the President of the Senate;—The President of the Senate shall, in presence of the Senate and House of Representatives, open all the certificates and the votes shall then be counted;——The person having the greatest number of votes for President, shall be the President, if such number be a majority of the whole number of Electors appointed; and if no person have such majority, then from the persons having the highest numbers not exceeding three on the list of those voted for as President, the House of Representatives shall choose immediately, by ballot, the President. But in choosing the President, the votes shall be taken by states, the representation from each state having one vote; a quorum for this purpose shall consist of a member or members from two-thirds of the states, and a majority of all the states shall be necessary to a choice. . . . The person having the greatest number of votes as Vice-President, shall be the Vice-President, if such number be a majority of the whole number of Electors appointed, and if no person have a majority, then from the two highest numbers on the list, the Senate shall choose the Vice-President; a quorum for the purpose shall consist of two-thirds of the whole number of Senators, and a majority of the whole number shall be necessary to a choice. But no person constitutionally ineligible to the office of President shall be eligible to that of Vice-President of the United States.

AMENDMENT XIII
Slavery abolished.
[Proposed by Congress, Jan. 31, 1865; ratified, Dec. 6, 1865.]
Neither slavery nor involuntary servitude, except as a punishment for crime whereof the party shall have been duly convicted, shall exist within the United States, or any place subject to their jurisdiction. . . .

AMENDMENT XIV
Rights of United States citizens.
[Proposed by the 39th Congress, June 13, 1866; ratified, July 9, 1868; declared to have been ratified in a proclamation by the secretary of state, July 28, 1868.]

1. All persons born or naturalized in the United States, and subject to the jurisdiction thereof, are citizens of the United States and of the State wherein they reside. No State shall make or enforce any law which shall abridge the privileges or immunities of citizens of the United States; nor shall any State deprive any person of life, liberty, or property, without due process of law; nor deny to any person within its jurisdiction the equal protection of the laws.

2. Representatives shall be apportioned among the several States according to their respective numbers, counting the whole number of persons in each State, excluding Indians not taxed. . . .

3. No person shall be a Senator or Representative in Congress, or elector of President and Vice-President, or hold any office, civil or military, under the United States, or under any State, who, having previously taken an oath, as a member of Congress, or as an officer of the United States, or as a member of any State legislature,

AMENDMENTS TO THE CONSTITUTION (CONT.)

or as an executive or judicial officer of any State, to support the Constitution of the United States, shall have engaged in insurrection or rebellion against the same, or given aid or comfort to the enemies thereof. But Congress may by a vote of two-thirds of each House, remove such disability. . . .

AMENDMENT XV

Race no bar to voting rights.

[Proposed by the 40th Congress, Feb. 26, 1869; ratified, Feb. 8, 1870.]

The right of citizens of the United States to vote shall not be denied or abridged by the United States or by any State on account of race, color, or previous condition of servitude. . . .

AMENDMENT XVI

Income taxes authorized.

[Proposed by Congress, July 12, 1909; ratified, Feb. 3, 1913.]

The Congress shall have power to lay and collect taxes on incomes, from whatever source derived, without apportionment among the several States, and without regard to any census or enumeration.

AMENDMENT XVII

United States senators to be elected by direct popular vote.

[Proposed by Congress, May 13, 1912; ratified, Apr. 8, 1913.]

The Senate of the United States shall be composed of two Senators from each State, elected by the people thereof, for six years; and each Senator shall have one vote. The electors in each State shall have the qualifications requisite for electors of the most numerous branch of the State legislatures. . . .

AMENDMENT XVIII

Prohibition established.

[Proposed by Congress, Dec. 18, 1917; ratified, Jan. 16, 1919. Repealed by Amendment XXI, effective Dec. 5, 1933.]

After one year from the ratification of this article the manufacture, sale, or transportation of intoxicating liquors within, the importation thereof into, or the exportation thereof from the United States and all territory subject to the jurisdiction thereof for beverage purposes is hereby prohibited. . . .

AMENDMENT XIX

Nationwide voting rights for women.

[Proposed by Congress, June 4, 1919; ratified, Aug. 18, 1920.]

The right of citizens of the United States to vote shall not be denied or abridged by the United States or by any State on account of sex. . . .

AMENDMENT XX

Terms of president and vice president to begin Jan. 20; those of senators, representatives, Jan. 3.

[Proposed by Congress, Mar. 2, 1932; ratified, Jan. 23, 1933.]

1. The terms of the President and Vice President shall end at noon on the 20th day of January, and the terms of Senators and Representatives at noon on the 3d day of January, of the years in which such terms would have ended if this article had not been ratified; and the terms of their successors shall then begin.

2. The Congress shall assemble at least once in every year, and such meeting shall begin at noon on the 3d day of January, unless they shall by law appoint a different day.

3. If, at the time fixed for the beginning of the term of the President, the President elect shall have died, the Vice President elect shall become President. If a President shall not have been chosen before the time fixed for the beginning of his term, or if the President elect shall have failed to qualify, then the Vice President elect shall act as President until a President shall have qualified; and the Congress may by law provide for the case wherein neither a President elect nor a Vice President elect shall have qualified, declaring who shall then act as President, or the manner in which one who is to act shall be selected, and such person shall act accordingly until a President or Vice President shall have qualified. . . .

AMENDMENT XXI

Prohibition (Amendment XVIII) repealed.

[Proposed by Congress, Feb. 20, 1933; ratified, Dec. 5, 1933.]

The eighteenth article of amendment to the Constitution of the United States is hereby repealed. . . .

AMENDMENT XXII

Presidential term limits.

[Proposed by Congress, Mar. 24, 1947; ratified, Feb. 27, 1951.]

No person shall be elected to the office of the President more than twice, and no person who has held the office of President, or acted as President, for more than two years of a term to which some other person was elected President shall be elected to the office of the President more than once. . . .

AMENDMENT XXIII
Presidential vote for District of Columbia.
[Proposed by Congress, June 16, 1960; ratified, Mar. 29, 1961.]
The District constituting the seat of Government of the United States shall appoint in such manner as the Congress may direct: A number of electors of President and Vice President equal to the whole number of Senators and Representatives in Congress to which the District would be entitled if it were a State, but in no event more than the least populous State; they shall be in addition to those appointed by the States, but they shall be considered, for the purposes of the election of President and Vice President, to be electors appointed by a State; and they shall meet in the District and perform such duties as provided by the twelfth article of amendment. . . .

AMENDMENT XXIV
Poll tax in federal elections abolished.
[Proposed by Congress, Aug. 27, 1962; ratified, Jan. 23, 1964.]
The right of citizens of the United States to vote in any primary or other election for President or Vice President, for electors for President or Vice President, or for Senator or Representative in Congress, shall not be denied or abridged by the United States or any State by reason of failure to pay any poll tax or other tax. . . .

AMENDMENT XXV
Presidential disability and succession.
[Proposed by Congress, July 6, 1965; ratified, Feb. 10, 1967.]
1. In case of the removal of the President from office or of his death or resignation, the Vice President shall become President.
2. Whenever there is a vacancy in the office of the Vice President, the President shall nominate a Vice President who shall take office upon confirmation by a majority vote of both houses of Congress.
3. Whenever the President transmits to the President pro tempore of the Senate and the Speaker of the House of Representatives his written declaration that he is unable to discharge the powers and duties of his office, and until he transmits to them a written declaration to the contrary, such powers and duties shall be discharged by the Vice President as Acting President.
4. Whenever the Vice President and a majority of either the principal officers of the executive departments or of such other body as

Congress may by law provide, transmit to the President pro tempore of the Senate and the Speaker of the House of Representatives their written declaration that the President is unable to discharge the powers and duties of his office, the Vice President shall immediately assume the powers and duties of the office as Acting President.

Thereafter, when the President transmits to the President pro tempore of the Senate and the Speaker of the House of Representatives his written declaration that no inability exists, he shall resume the powers and duties of his office unless the Vice President and a majority of either the principal officers of the executive department or of such other body as Congress may by law provide, transmit within four days to the President pro tempore of the Senate and the Speaker of the House of Representatives their written declaration that the President is unable to discharge the powers and duties of his office. Thereupon Congress shall decide the issue, assembling within forty-eight hours for that purpose if not in session. If the Congress, within twenty-one days after receipt of the latter written declaration, or, if Congress is not in session, within twenty-one days after Congress is required to assemble, determines by two-thirds vote of both Houses that the President is unable to discharge the powers and duties of his office, the Vice President shall continue to discharge the same as Acting President; otherwise, the President shall resume the powers and duties of his office.

AMENDMENT XXVI
Nationwide voting age lowered to eighteen.
[Proposed by Congress, Mar. 23, 1971; ratified, June 30, 1971.]
The right of citizens of the United States, who are eighteen years of age or older, to vote shall not be denied or abridged by the United States or by any State on account of age. . . .

AMENDMENT XXVII
Congressional pay.
[Proposed by Congress, Sept. 25, 1789; ratified, May 7, 1992.]
No law, varying the compensation for the services of the Senators and Representatives, shall take effect, until an election of Representatives shall have intervened.

SOURCE: The World Almanac and Book of Facts 2003

1776	Virginia Declaration of Rights adopted, June 12. American Declaration of Independence issued, July 4.
1787	Constitutional Convention holds first formal meeting in Philadelphia, May 25. Delegates sign Constitution, September 17.
1789	Constitution takes effect, March 4. Bill of Rights approved by Congress and submitted to the states, September 25.
1791	Bill of Rights ratified, December 15.
1804	Method of choosing the president and vice president changed (Amendment XII ratified).
1865	With the end of the Civil War (1861–65), Amendment XIII abolishes slavery.
1868	Meaning of United States citizenship defined (Amendment XIV ratified).
1913	Federal income tax established (Amendment XVI ratified). Direct election of United States senators required (Amendment XVII ratified).
1919	Prohibition established (Amendment XVIII ratified). Liquor sales barred as of 1920; repealed 1933 with passage of Amendment XXI.
1920	Women guaranteed right to vote (Amendment XIX ratified).
1951	President limited to two terms in office (Amendment XXII ratified).
1961	District of Columbia gets presidential vote (Amendment XXIII ratified).
1964	Poll tax abolished (Amendment XXIV ratified).
1967	Rules for presidential disability and succession spelled out (Amendment XXV ratified).
1971	Voting age lowered to eighteen (Amendment XXVI ratified).
1982	Equal Rights Amendment fails.
1992	Congressional pay raises limited (Amendment XXVII ratified).

GLOSSARY

amendments: changes made to the original United States Constitution.

bail: money paid to ensure that someone arrested and then released from jail will actually show up for trial.

Bill of Rights: the first ten amendments to the U.S. Constitution.

Civil War: a war (1861–65) between northern and southern states that began when the South (Confederacy) rebelled against the Union. Slavery in the South was a major cause of the conflict, which was won by the North.

double jeopardy: putting someone on trial twice for the same crime.

due process: fair treatment under the law.

Equal Protection Clause: the part of the Fourteenth Amendment that requires state governments to provide equal legal protection for all.

Equal Rights Amendment (ERA): a constitutional amendment that would guarantee women the same legal rights as men; passed by Congress but not ratified.

Establishment Clause: the part of the First Amendment that prevents Congress from setting up an official national religion.

exclusionary rule: the idea that wrongfully obtained evidence cannot be used against someone who is being tried for a crime.

federal government: the government of the United States.

framers: a name for the group of political leaders who wrote the United States Constitution.

libeled: damaged someone's reputation by publishing false information.

militias: groups of armed citizens.

poll tax: a tax that people had to pay in order to be allowed to vote.

Prohibition: a period (1920–33) in American history when the Eighteenth Amendment outlawed the making and selling of alcoholic beverages.

ratified: approved by the states.

search warrant: a legal document that allows police officers to enter someone's home and collect evidence they find there.

secular: nonreligious.

segregation: separation of one racial group from another, enforced by law.

suffrage: the right to vote.

TO FIND OUT MORE

BOOKS

Alderman, Ellen, and Caroline Kennedy.
In Our Defense: The Bill of Rights in Action.
New York: William Morrow, 1991.

Alderman, Ellen, and Caroline Kennedy.
The Right to Privacy.
New York: Knopf, 1995.

Hudson, David L.
The Fourteenth Amendment: Equal Protection Under the Law.
Berkeley Heights, N.J.: Enslow, 2002.

Monroe, Judy.
The Nineteenth Amendment: Women's Right to Vote.
Springfield, N.J.: Enslow, 1998.

Morin, Isobel V.
Our Changing Constitution: How and Why We Have Amended It.
Brookfield, Conn.: Millbrook Press, 1998.

Patrick, John J.
Bill of Rights: A History in Documents.
New York: Oxford University Press, 2003.

Streissguth, Thomas.
Gun Control: The Pros and Cons.
Berkeley Heights, N.J.: Enslow, 2001.

INTERNET SITES

American Civil Liberties Union
http://www.aclu.org/
Organization dedicated to defending the Bill of Rights.

The Charters of Freedom
http://www.archives.gov/exhibit_hall/charters_of_freedom/charters_of_freedom.html
United States government site maintained by the National Archives and Records Administration.

FindLaw Legal News
http://news.findlaw.com/
Detailed coverage of legal issues.

The United States Constitution Online
http://www.usconstitution.net/
Useful links to other sites.

INDEX

Page numbers in *italic* type refer to illustration captions.

INDEX (CONT.)